Little Blue Dot

2

Margaret Whitfield

Activity Book

OXFORD
UNIVERSITY PRESS

MODULE	UNIT	VOCABULARY	STRUCTURES	PHONICS	VALUES & FUNCTIONAL LANGUAGE	NUMBERS	EXPLORE	PROJECT
	Unit 1 Senses p.6 **Generalization:** *We use our senses to explore.*	see, hear, feel, smell, taste horse, duck, frog, mouse cow, sheep, chicken, donkey	I can (see) a (bird). I can (hear) something. Can you (see) a (duck)? Yes, I can. / No, I can't.	CVC words with **a** (bat, hat)	**Be patient** Wait a minute.	Review 1–10	On the farm	Make animal masks.
Let's explore p.4 Concept: *exploration* Level 1 review fingers	**Unit 2 Food** p.16 **Generalization:** *We use all our senses to give us information about the food we eat.*	potatoes, peas, tomatoes, onions, carrots lemon, pineapple, kiwi, grape healthy, cookies, chips	Do you like (potatoes)? Yes, I do. / No, I don't. Is it (a kiwi)? Yes, it is. / No, it isn't.	CVC words with **e** (bed) and **i** (dig)	**Eat fruit and vegetables** Would you like (a carrot)? Yes, please. / No, thank you.	11, 12	Healthy eating	Make and share pretend food.
	Unit 3 Weather p.26 **Generalization:** *The weather affects us and things around us.*	sunny, rainy, cloudy, windy, snowy hot, cold, wet, dry rainbow, bubbles, puddle, ice	What's the weather like? It's (sunny). He's/She's (cold). He/She isn't (cold).	CVC words with **o** (log) and **u** (tub)	**Be careful in the sun** Put on your hat. Okay.	13, 14	Weather experiments	Make a weather picture.

Now I know Units 1–3 project p.36

Story time: The picnic p.38

MODULE	UNIT	VOCABULARY	STRUCTURES	PHONICS	VALUES & FUNCTIONAL LANGUAGE	NUMBERS	EXPLORE	PROJECT
Where are we? p.40 Concept: *location* apartment house, street, school	**Unit 4 My home** p.42 **Generalization:** *Homes can be very different, but we use them to do similar things.*	bedroom, kitchen, living room, bathroom, dining room hide and seek, spider, wardrobe eat, wash, sleep, play hive, nest, web	Where are you? I'm in the (bedroom). There you are. What are you doing? I'm (sleeping).	CVC words with **ck** (sock) and **x** (fox)	**Play together** Let's play together! Good idea.	15, 16	Animal homes	Make birds and nests.
	Unit 5 My school p.52 **Generalization:** *We do things in different places.*	table, chair, rug, under, on read, write, color, talk classroom, schoolyard, board	Where's the (hat)? It's on / under the (table). Look at this! Are you (reading)? Yes, I am. / No, I'm not.	CVC words with **sh** (ship, dish)	**Take care of your toys** Our toys are dirty. Let's wash them.	17, 18	At school	Make a classroom picture.

MODULE	UNIT	VOCABULARY	STRUCTURES	PHONICS	VALUES & FUNCTIONAL LANGUAGE	NUMBERS	EXPLORE	PROJECT
Where are we? p.40 Concept: *location* apartment house, street, school	**Unit 6 My town** p.62 **Generalization:** *We visit different places for different reasons.*	park, toy store, zoo, swimming pool, supermarket map, river, bridge	Where is he/she? She's/He's at the (park). Where's my mom? That isn't my mom! There's a (park). It's in front of / behind / next to the (supermarket). It's between the (swimming pool) and the (park).	CVC words with **ch** (chips, chick) and **tch** (hatch, catch)	**Try again** Let's try again.	19, 20	Maps	Make a town.
	Now I know Units 4–6 project p.72							
	Story time: The noisy boat **p.74**							
Changes p.76 Concept: *changes* man, woman, young, old	**Unit 7 My body** p.78 **Generalization:** *Our bodies change over time.*	body, neck, arms, hands, feet paint glasses, teeth, hair, beard brushing, drinking, wiping	This is my (body). These are my (arms). He/She has (hair). He/She doesn't have (a beard).	CVC words with **ng** (long, ring)	**Wash your hands** I need to wash my hands. My hands are clean.	Review 1–20: measuring	Personal care	Make a photos timeline.
	Unit 8 Day and night p.88 **Generalization:** *We do different things at different times of day.*	wake up, get dressed, go to school, go to sleep, take a shower in the morning, in the afternoon, in the evening, at night moon, star, raccoon	I (wake up). Let's (read a story). When do you (brush your teeth)? In the (morning). / At night.	CVC words with unvoiced **th** (moth, path)	**Sleep time** It's time to go to sleep. Good night.	Review 1–20: missing numbers	Nighttime	Make a daily activities flip-book.
	Unit 9 Clothes p.98 **Generalization:** *We change into different clothes for different situations.*	shorts, pants, skirt, shoes, T-shirt party, costume, paper, make jacket, sweater, scarf, dress pajamas, swimsuit, apron	I'm/He's/She's wearing (a T-shirt). His/Her (sweater) is too big / small.	CVC words with voiced **th** (this, that)	**Reuse things** We can reuse this (shoe).	Review 1–20: compare before / after	Clothes for activities	Make a favorite clothes picture.
	Now I know Units 7–9 project p.108							
	Story time: Elsa's favorite dress **p.110**							

Let's explore

1 Look and match. 2 Circle the things you can say.

1 🔊001 Listen, follow, and say.　2 Circle the letters in your name.

1 Senses

1 Count, write, and say.

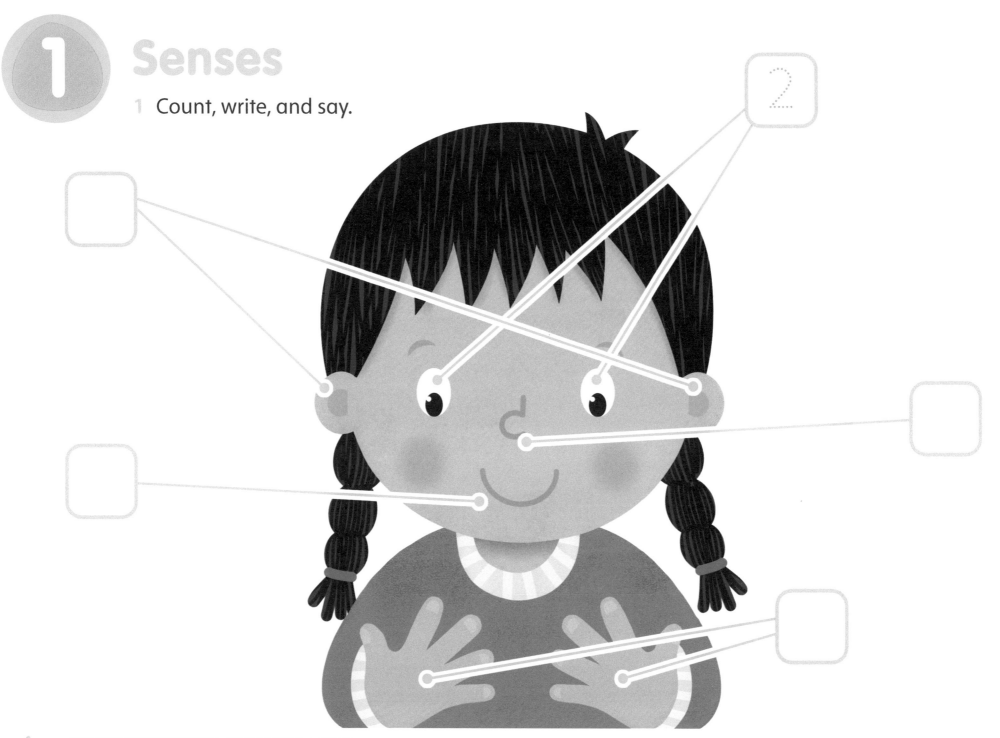

1 🔊002 Listen and match.   2 Read and circle.

(see) hear   see   smell   taste   feel   hear   taste   smell   feel

1 🔊003 Listen and point.　　2 Trace and say.　　3 Follow.

bag

bat

cat

hat

dad

Lesson 3 Phonics　　**Language focus:** CVC words with *a* (*bat, hat*)

1 What's different in picture 2? Circle five things.

2 Trace, read, and circle.

It's a hat.

It's a bat.

1 Circle the children who are waiting. **2** Trace.

I can wait.

Lesson 5 Value   **Value:** be patient   **Language focus:** *Wait a minute.*

1 Trace.   2 Look at the number and draw.

1   2   3   4   5   6   7   8   9   10

5

3

7

9

1 🔊 004 Listen, circle, and say.   2 Trace.

duck

⬤ Yes, I can.   No, I can't.

horse

Yes, I can.   No, I can't.

mouse

Yes, I can.   No, I can't.

frog

Yes, I can.   No, I can't.

1 Trace and join. 2 Look and color.

cow   sheep   chicken   donkey

1 Look, read, and match.

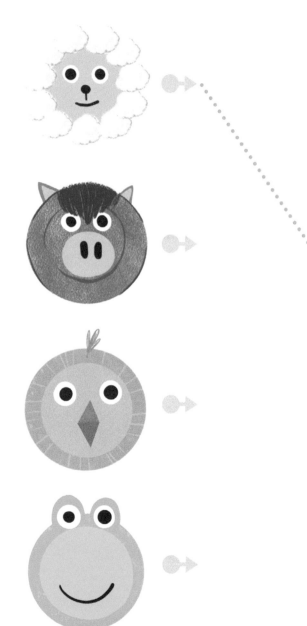

horse

frog

sheep

chicken

Language focus: *I can see / hear a (sheep).*

1 Find and check ✓.   2 🔊005 Listen and draw.

cat ✓   duck ☐   donkey ☐   horse  ☐

frog ☐   cow  ☐   chicken ☐   mouse ☐

Food

1 What do you like? Look, join, and say.   2 Circle your favorite.

bread

bananas

noodles

salad

cheese

milk

1 Look, read, and color.   2   ◀))006 Listen and trace. Say *Yes, I do* or *No, I don't.*

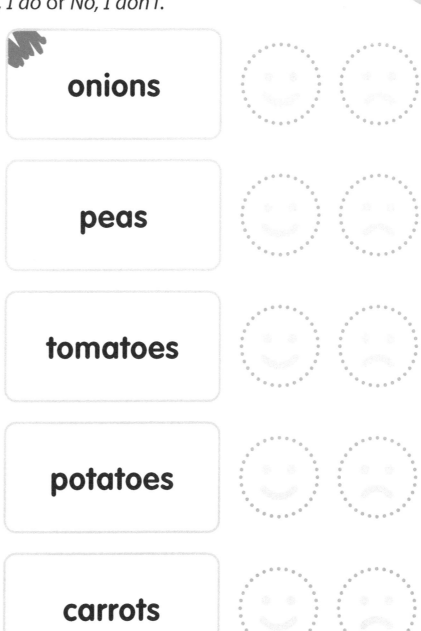

onions

peas

tomatoes

potatoes

carrots

1 🔊007 Listen and point. 2 Match and write **e** or **i**.

bed **dig** **red** **ten** **big**

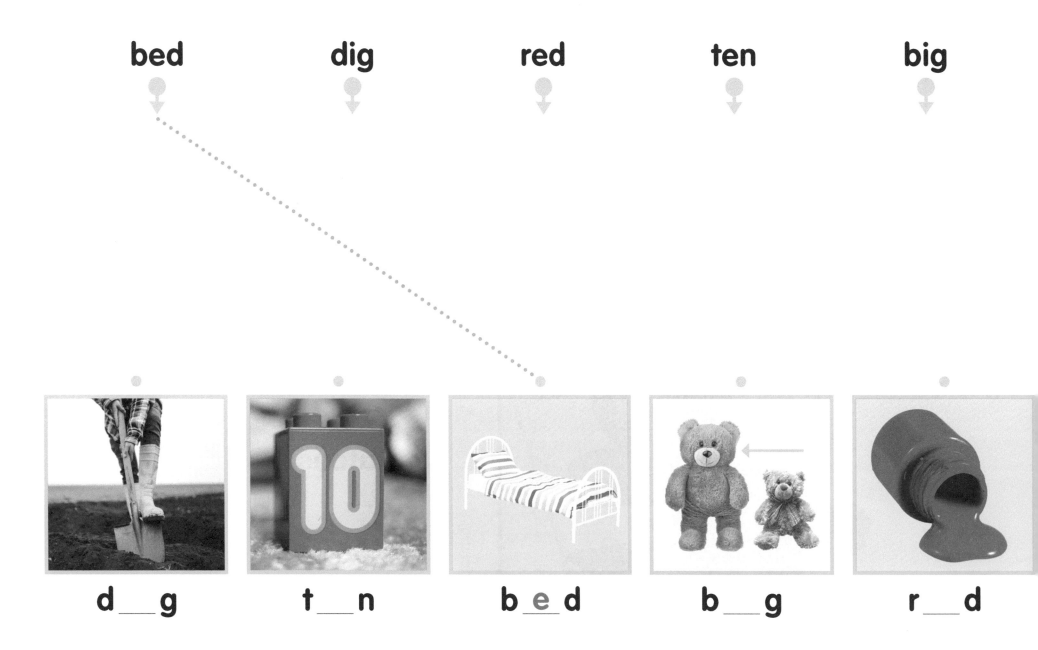

d __ g t __ n b _e_ d b __ g r __ d

1 Look and match.

2 Circle the foods in the omelet.

eggs　　　**potatoes**　　　**carrots**　　　**tomatoes**

2

1 Choose **one** from each pair and color.   2 Ask and answer.   3 Trace.

an apple

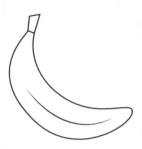

a banana

a mango

watermelon

a carrot

a tomato

peas

salad

I eat fruit and vegetables.

1 Count and trace.

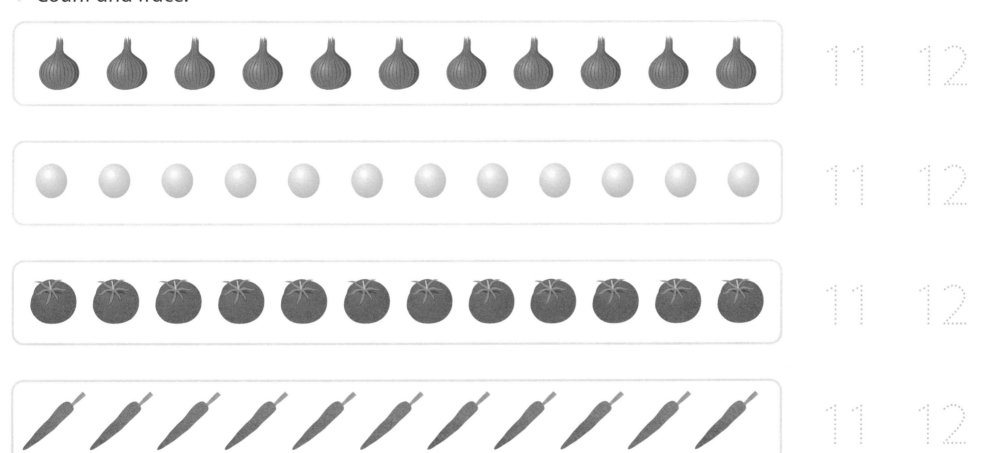

2 Draw.

12

2

1 Look and match.　2  008 Listen and answer.　3 Trace.

①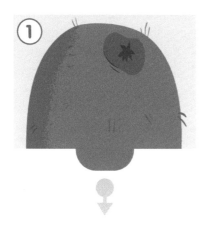

②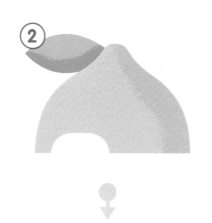

③

④

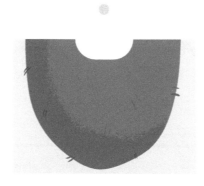

pineapple　　kiwi　　grape　　lemon

Lesson 7 Song　　**Language focus:** *Is it a kiwi / grape / lemon / pineapple? Yes, it is. / No, it isn't.*

1 🔊 009 Listen and color. 2 Circle the snack that **isn't** healthy.

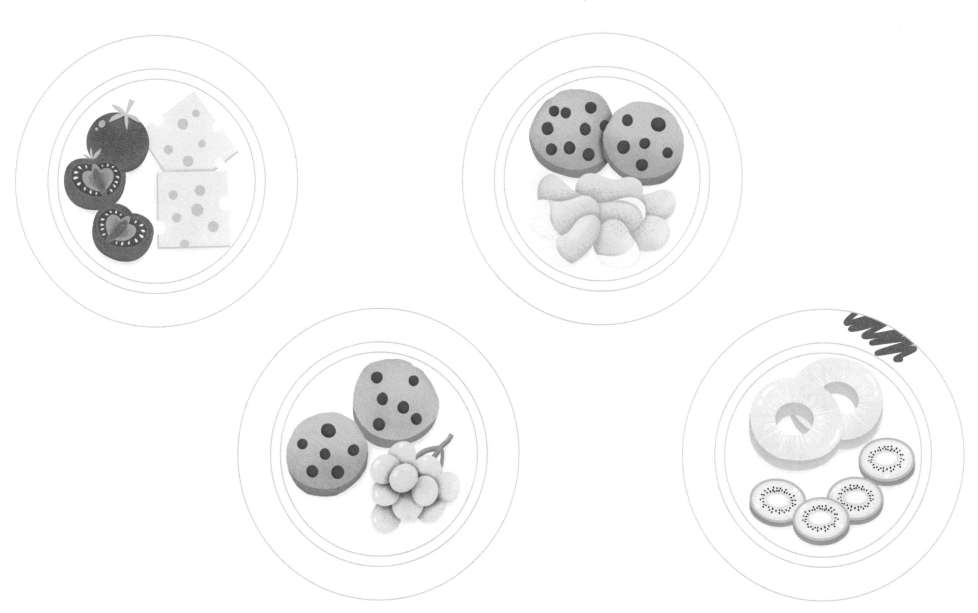

1 Read and match.   **2** Draw what's missing.

peas

pineapple

tomatoes

grapes

carrots

kiwi

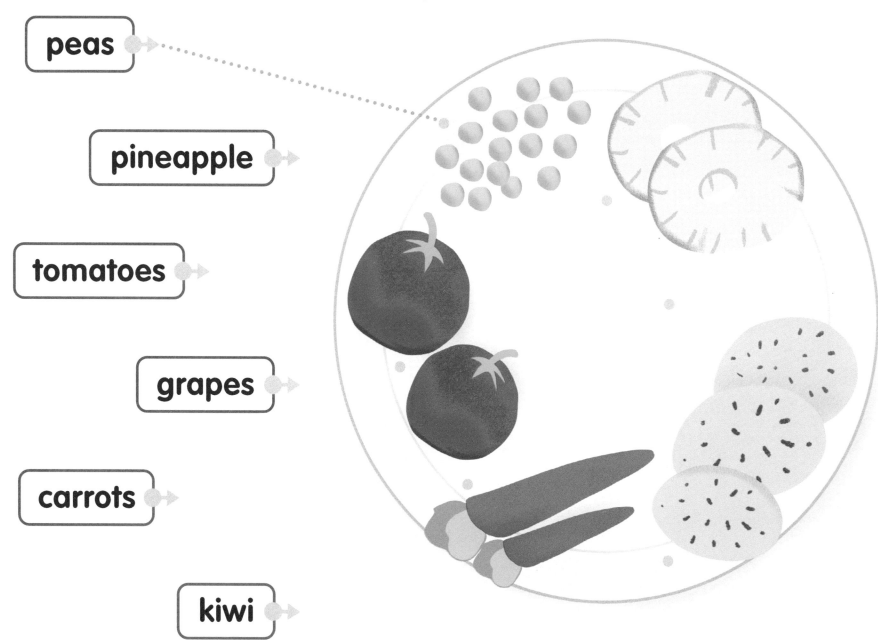

   Language focus: *Do you like (kiwis)? Yes, I do. / No, I don't. Would you like some (peas)? Yes, please. / No, thank you.*

1 What's next? Draw and circle.

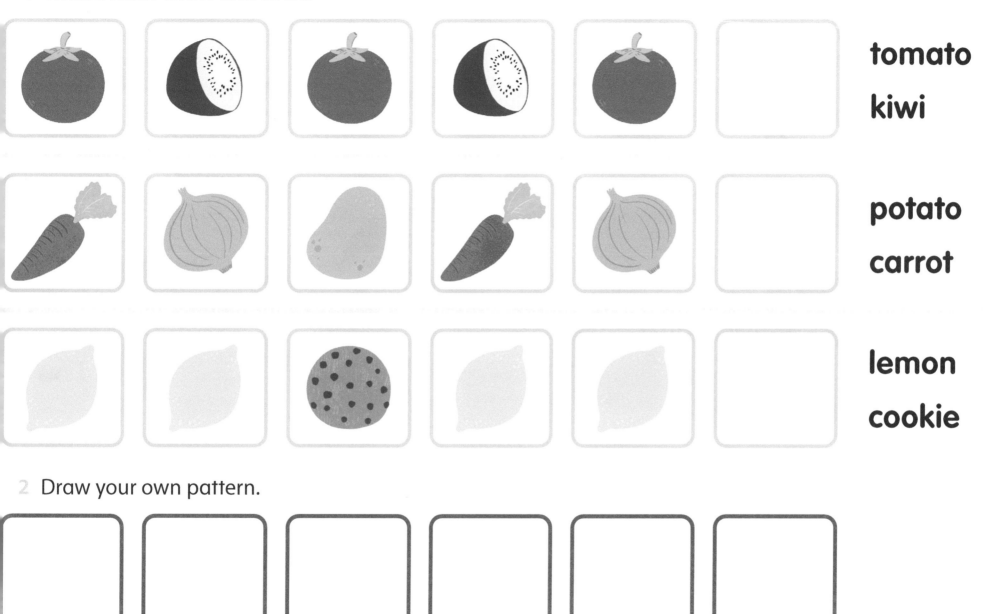

tomato
kiwi

potato
carrot

lemon
cookie

2 Draw your own pattern.

 **Weather**

1 Find and write **A** or **B**.

 **sun** A

 umbrella

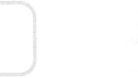 **fish**

 frog

 kite

 hat

1 Trace and color. 2 🔊010 Listen and number.

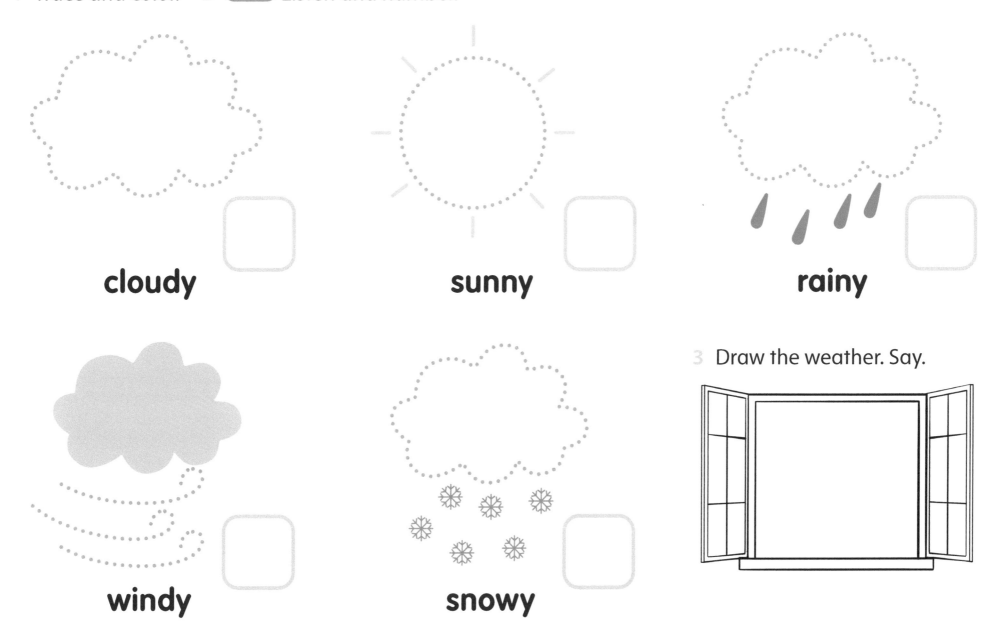

cloudy

sunny

rainy

windy

snowy

3 Draw the weather. Say.

3

1 🔊011 Listen and circle **o** or **u**.   2 Match and trace.

o u   o u   o u   o u   o u

dog   log   mom   run   tub

1 Look and color.

3

1 Draw hats on the children playing outside.

2 Draw your hat. **3** Trace.

I'm careful in the sun.

Lesson 5 Value   **Value:** be careful in the sun   **Language focus:** *Put on your hat. Okay.*

1 Connect the numbers.   2 Draw **14** raindrops.

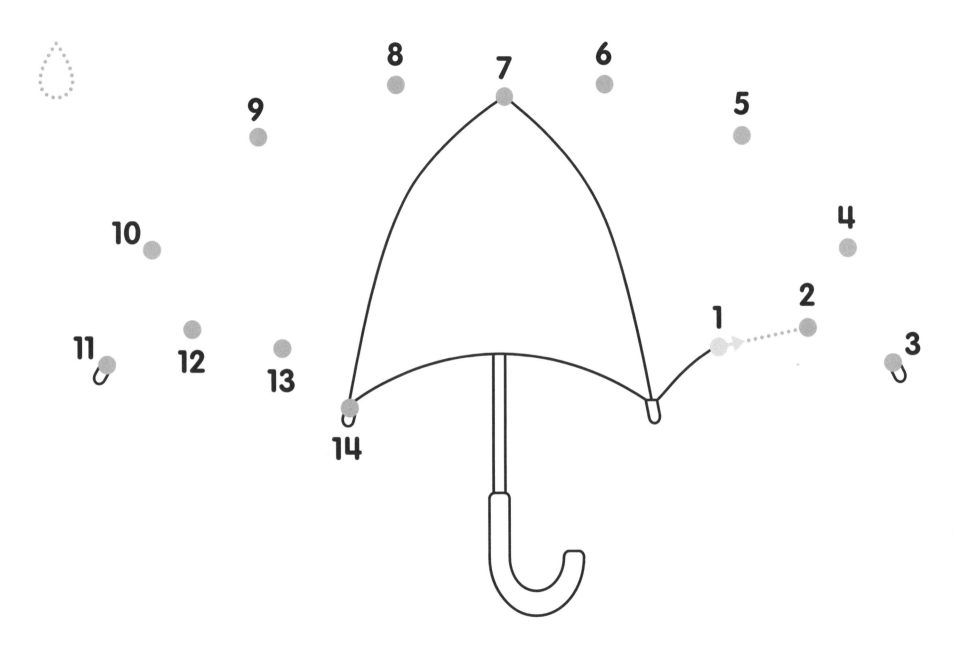

3

1 🔊012 Listen and color.   2 Trace.

hot   wet   dry   cold

1 Draw and color.   2 Trace.

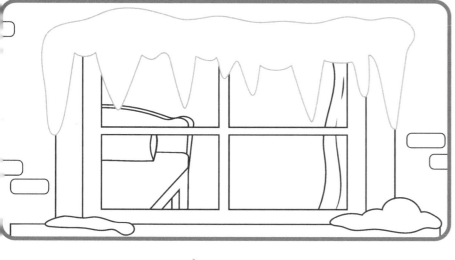

ice

bubbles

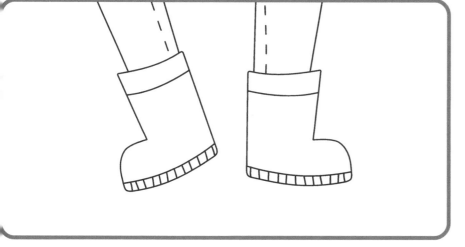

a puddle

a rainbow

1 Look, read, and match.

 **sunny**

 **windy**

 **rainy**

snowy

Lesson 9 Project   **Language focus:** *What's the weather like? It's (rainy).*

1 🔊013 **Listen and number.** 2 🔊014 **Listen again and circle.**

1 What can you explore? Match.

1 Color the things that make you happy.　　**2** Circle the things that make your friend happy.

bubbles

puddles

cookies

peas

ducks

frogs

1 Draw the weather. Color.

It's sunny today.

Izzy can see gray clouds.

Now, it's rainy.

2 Do you like the story? Color.

No, I don't. | 1 | 2 | 3 | 4 | 5 | 6 | 7 | 8 | 9 | 10 | **Yes, I do.**

1 Draw yourself on a picnic.

Where are we?

1 Look and match.

2 Read, find, and circle. What else can you see?

grapes　　　**a tub**　　　**carrots**　　　**a duck**

Lesson 1 Concept　　**Units 4–6 concept:** location　　**Language focus:** *apartment, house, street, school*

1 Draw your home.

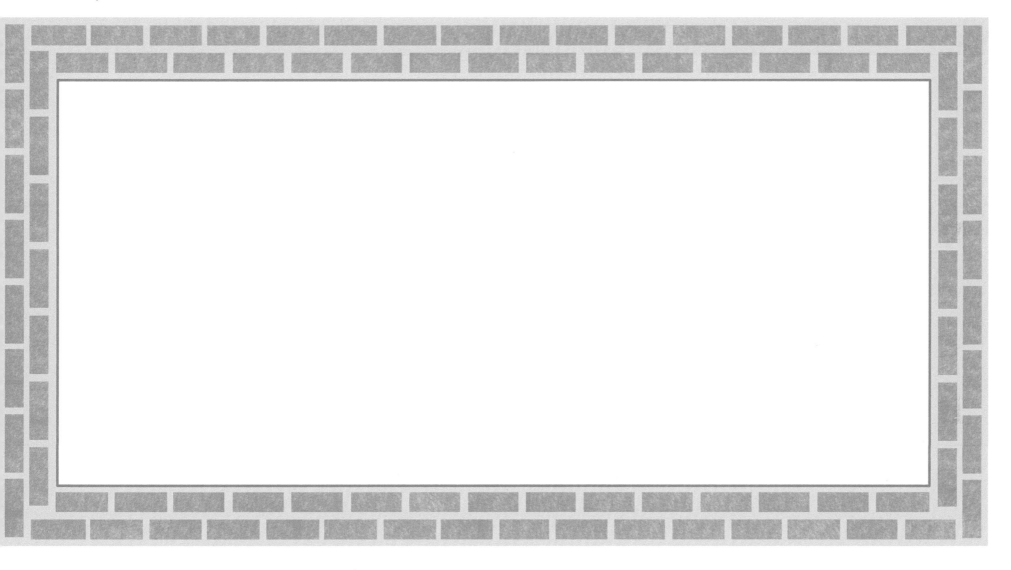

2 Read and circle.

This is my apartment.   **This is my house.**

My home

1 Circle the home most like yours. **2** Check ✓ the home you would like to live in.

1 Look, read, and match.   **2** 🔊015 Listen and repeat.

living room

dining room

kitchen

bathroom

bedroom

4

1 Look and match.　**2** 016 Listen and trace.

ck

x

fox　　　sock　　　duck　　　box

3 Read and circle.

The fox is in the box.

Lesson 3 Phonics　　**Language focus:** CVC words with *ck* (*sock*), *x* (*fox*)

1 Find and circle. **2** Say.

 **a fox**

 **a sock**

 **a duck**

bathroom

bedroom

1 Color the children playing together. **2** Trace.

We play together.

Lesson 5 Value   **Value:** play together   **Language focus:** *Let's play together! Good idea.*

1 Count and trace.

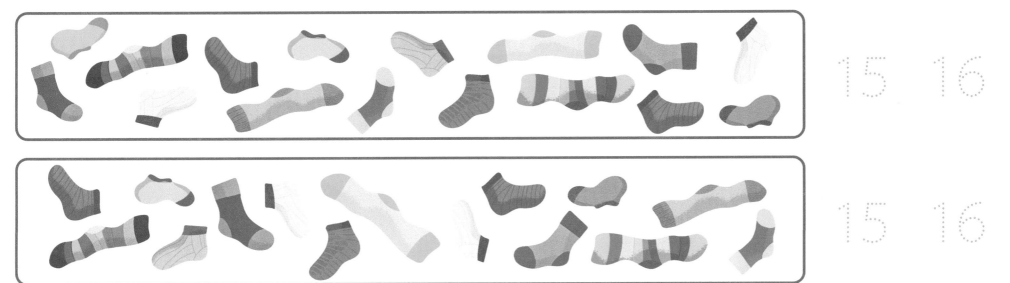

15 16

15 16

2 Look at the number and draw more socks.

15

16

1 🔊017 Look and read. Listen and check ✓.　　**2** Trace.

I'm washing. ☐

I'm eating. ✓

I'm sleeping. ☐

I'm playing. ☐

I'm washing. ☐

I'm sleeping. ☐

I'm playing. ☐

I'm eating. ☐

Lesson 7 Song　　**Language focus:** *What are you doing? I'm eating / washing / sleeping / playing.*

1 Join the animals with their homes. **2** Trace.

web   hive   nest

4

1 Look and match. **2** Color the birds.

3 Read and point.

I'm a yellow and black bird. I'm eating.

Lesson 9 Project   **Language focus:** *nest, bird, I'm sleeping.*

1 🔊018 Listen and match.

2 Read and color.

 **dining room**   **bathroom**   **living room**   **bedroom**   **kitchen**

5 My school

1 Trace and say the things you do in school.

wash

eat

sleep

run

play

sing

swim

talk

1 🔊 **019** Listen and draw.   **2** Write.

① chair

② table

③ rug

④ t__ble

⑤ chai__

3 Read and color.

The red hat is on the rug.

1 Read and circle. **2** 🔊020 Listen and say.

dish   Ash

fish   ship

ship   Ash

fish   dish

3 Trace, read, and color.

Ash **is on the** ship .

1 What's in the story? Color and trace.

duck

ship

bag

fish

sock

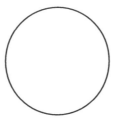
ball

frog

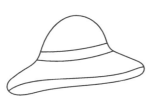
hat

fox

2 Draw a tower and say.

1 Join the toys with the box. Say. **2** Trace.

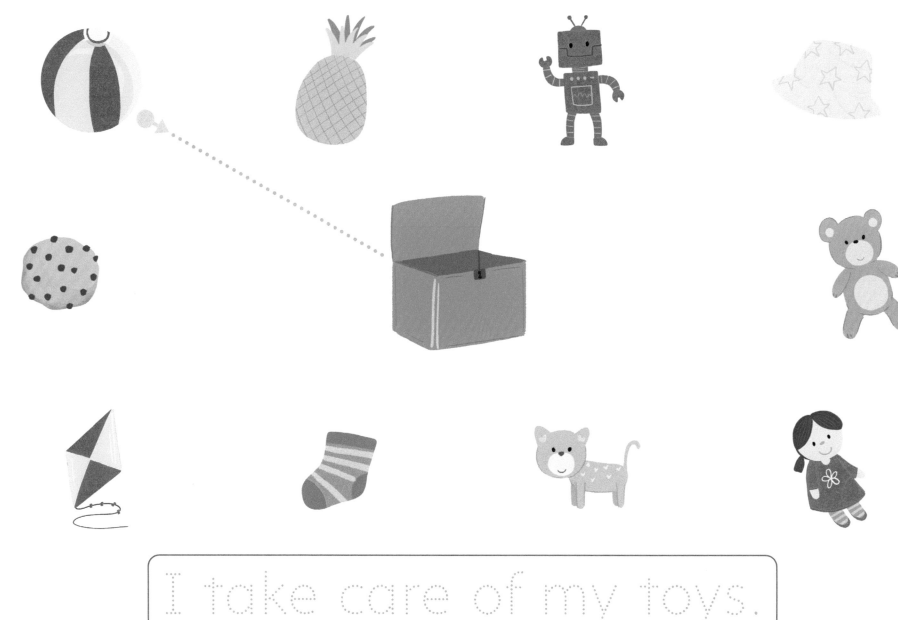

I take care of my toys.

1 Connect and say the numbers.

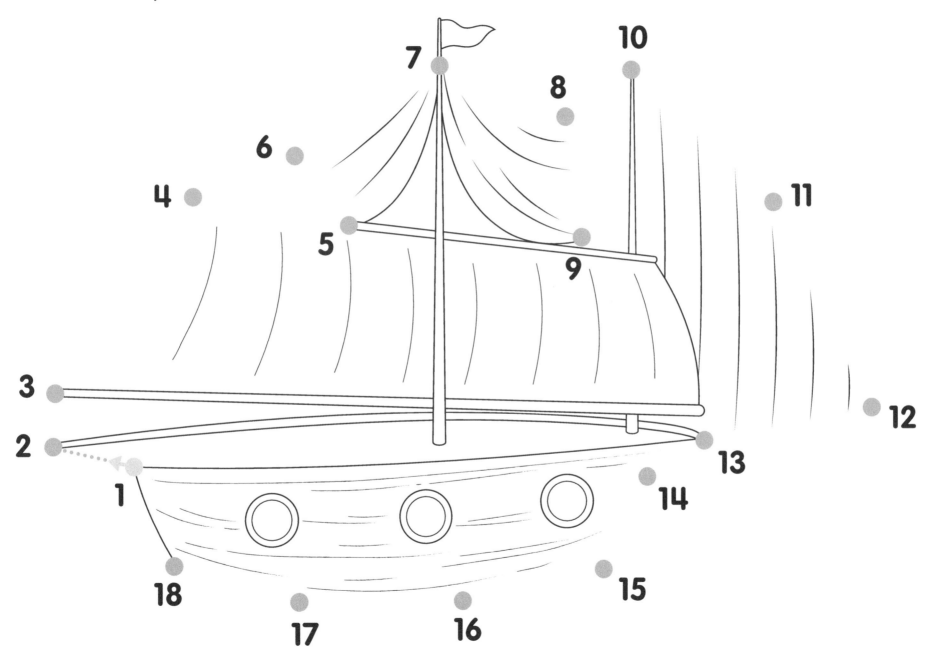

5

1 🔊 021 Listen and match.   **2** Trace.

①

②

③

④

Yes, I am.

writing   reading   coloring   talking

Lesson 7 Song   **Language focus:** *Are you reading / writing / coloring / talking? Yes, I am. / No, I'm not.*

1 Find, circle, and say.　**2** Trace.

classroom　　schoolyard　　board

1 What's different in picture 2? Circle six things and say.

2 Read and circle.

The bag is on the table. I'm reading.

1 Read and match.

table   **rug**   **board**

2 🔊022 Listen and draw.

My town

1 Look, read, and circle. **2** What do you do on the weekend? Draw and say.

swim   **talk**

wash   **eat**

play   **read**

sleep   **walk**

run   **look**

1 🔊023 Listen and match.

2 Read and circle.

She's at the toy store.

He's at the zoo.

6

1 🔊024 Listen and circle the **ch** words.

2 Look, read, and write. **3** 🔊025 Listen and repeat.

catch chicks

I can ca__ __ __.

Six __ __icks.

1 Circle Chip's mom.

2 Look and match.

Language focus: *That isn't my mom!* **Lesson 4** Story **65**

6

1 Look and match.   **2** Point and say *Try again!*   **3** Trace.

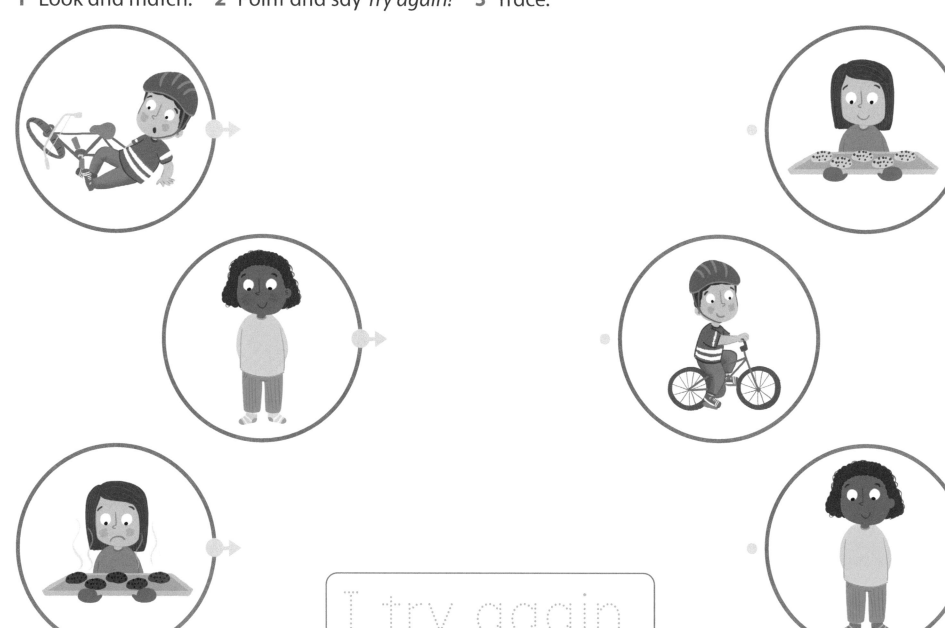

I try again.

Lesson 5 Value   **Value:** try again   **Language focus:** *Let's try again.*

1 Look and color.

17   18   19   20

2 Count the chicks and write.

1 🔊026 Listen and number.　**2** Trace.

  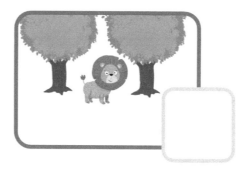 

in front of　behind　between　next to

3 Look, read, and color. Say where the places are.

There's a park. ◯

There's a zoo. ◯

There's a toy store. ◯

There's a school. ◯

There's a supermarket. ◯

There's a swimming pool. ◯

Lesson 7 Song　　**Language focus:** *There's a park. It's in front of / behind / between / next to the zoo (and the supermarket).*

1 🔊027 Listen and match.   **2** Trace and say.

river

bridge

6

1 Look, read, and match.   **2** Point and say.

river

toy store

zoo

park

swimming pool

supermarket

1 Where are they? Look, guess, and say.　**2** 🔊028 Listen and trace.

park

toy store

toy store

zoo

supermarket

swimming pool

supermarket

river

zoo

river

park

toy store

Where are we? Now I know

1 🔊 029 Listen and say the number. **2** Where do you do these things? Match and say.

①  ② ③  ④  ⑤ ⑥

at home

in school

at the park

1 What's in your classroom? Check ✔ and color.　**2** Trace.

a board　　a rug　　chairs　　tables

windows　　a door　　a shelf　　a box

1 Match. Read and write the missing letters.

 **duck**

 **bee**

 **frog**

The f__ __ __ is in the living room.

The d__ __ __ is in the bathroom.

The b__ __ is in the kitchen.

2 Do you like the story? Color.

No, I don't. ☹ | 1 | 2 | 3 | 4 | 5 | 6 | 7 | 8 | 9 | 10 | ☺ **Yes, I do.**

1 Draw yourself on the boat. Say.

Where are you?
What are you doing?

Changes

1 🔊030 Listen and number.　　2 Point and say.

1

3 Read, find, and circle. What else can you see?

a sock　　a shoe　　a table　　a rug　　a school

Lesson 1 Concept　　**Units 7–9 concept:** changes　　**Language focus:** *man, woman, young, old*

1 Choose **two** people from your family. Circle and draw.   2 Read and color.

grandpa   **dad**   **brother**   **grandma**   **mom**   **sister**

He's a | man. | boy.   She's a | woman. | girl.

7 My body

1 Match.   2 Write the missing letters.

girl

woman

man

boy

m __ __

b __ __

w __ __ __ __

g i r l

1 🔊031 Listen, read, and match.

neck ●➡

body ●➡

arms ●➡

hands ●➡

feet ●➡

2 Look and write.

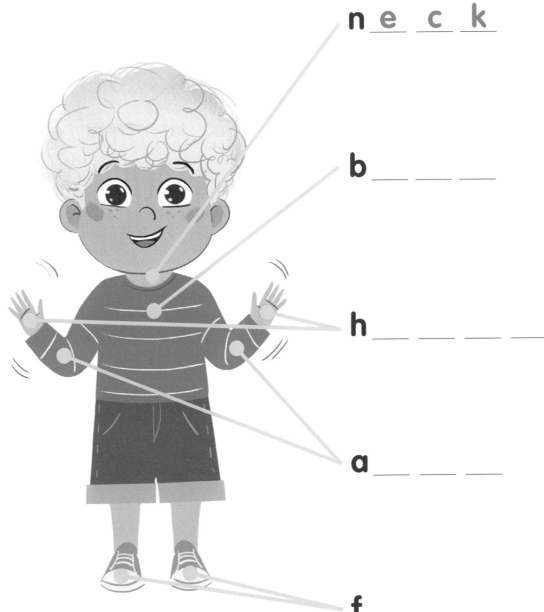

n e c k

b_ _ _ _

h_ _ _ _ _

a_ _ _ _

f_ _ _ _

7

1 🔊032 Listen, trace, and say.　　**2** Look and match.

 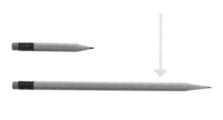  

3 Read and draw.

A big ring.

1 Look and match.

What are you doing?

These are my wings.

This is my foot.

2 Look and color.

7 1 Look and number. 2 Trace.

I wash my hands.

Lesson 5 Value   **Value:** wash your hands   **Language focus:** *I need to wash my hands. My hands are clean.*

1 Trace and say. Write and say the next number.

1 🔊033 Listen and circle.   2 Talk about the other pictures.

3 Trace. Read and point.

He has a beard.
He doesn't have hair.

She has 2 teeth.
She has glasses.

Lesson 7 Song   Language focus: He/She has/doesn't have glasses / teeth / hair / a beard.

1 Match and say. 2 Write.

brushing

brushing

drinking

wiping

I'm
w____ ____ ____ ____ ____
my mouth.

I'm
b r u s h i n g
my teeth.

I'm
d____ ____ ____ ____ ____ ____
water.

I'm
b____ ____ ____ ____ ____
my hair.

7

1 🔊034 Listen, find, and write.

3

2 Read and circle.

He has glasses.

Language focus: *I'm sleeping. I have/don't have teeth / hair / glasses. These are my arms / hands / feet.*

1 Read, find, and write.   2 Color to match.

This is my
b ___ ___ ___ ___.

These are my
___ ___ ___ ___.

These are my
___ ___ ___ ___ ___.

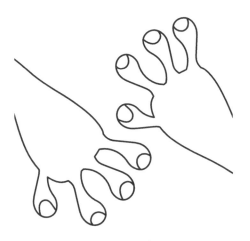

hands

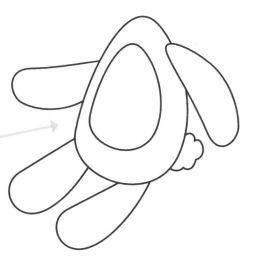

body

feet

8 Day and night

1 Look and match.

2 Read and find. What else can you see?

bed   **fox**   **hat**   **rug**   **sun**

1 🔊035 Listen and number.   2 Read and match.

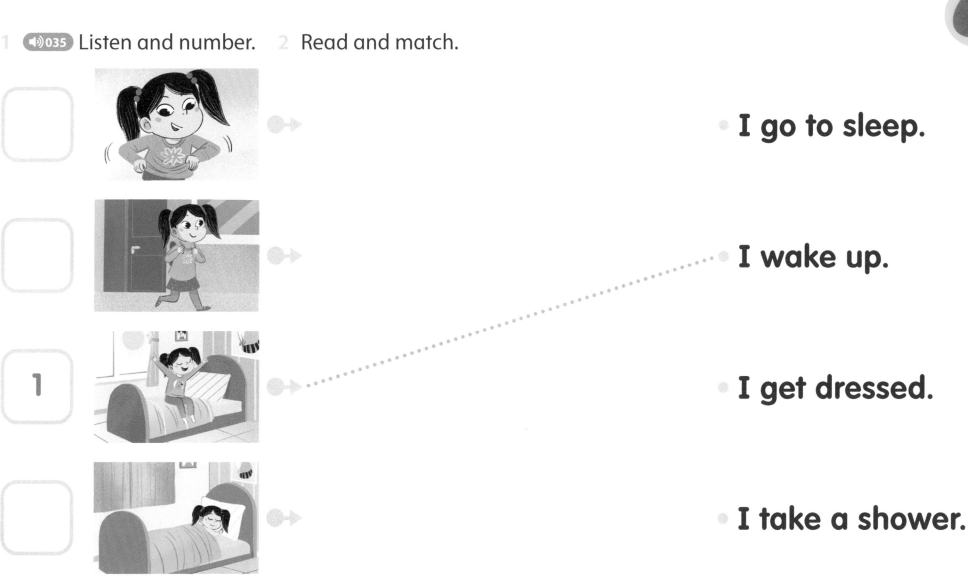

I go to sleep.

I wake up.

I get dressed.

I take a shower.

I go to school.

1 🔊036 Listen and write.

ch f th s

_f_ **ox**   ___**ock**   ___ ___**ick**   **mo**___ ___

2 Follow and say.

1 What happens in the story? Remember and circle.

2 Color the picture of Spark feeling tired.

8 1 Check ✓ the things you do before you go to sleep. Say. 2 Draw one more. 3 Trace.

I can go to sleep by myself.

Lesson 5 Value   **Value:** sleep time   **Language focus:** *It's time to go to sleep. Good night.*

1 Count and write.   2 Say the numbers in order.

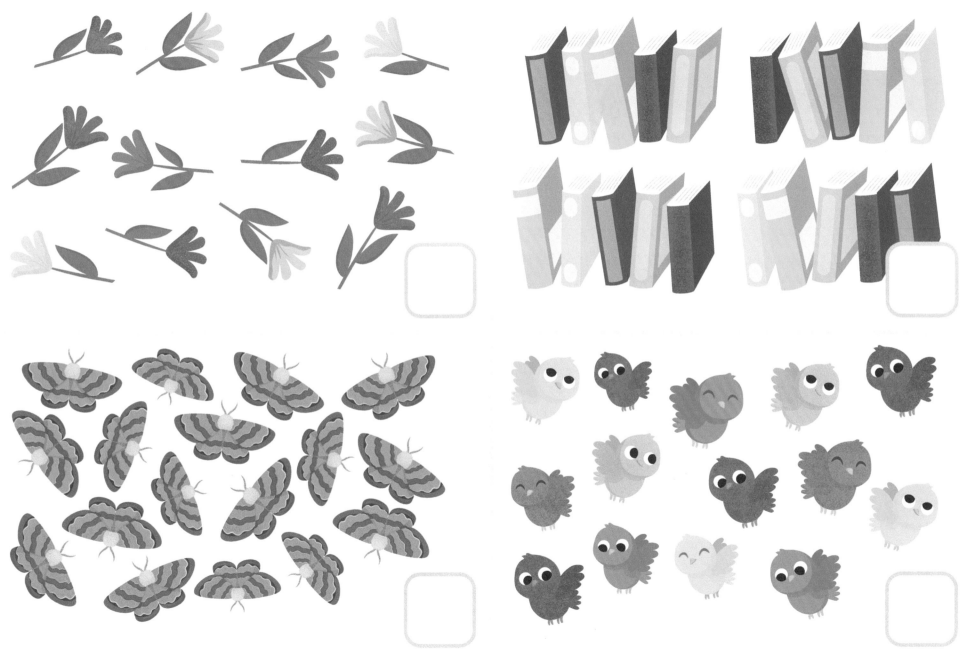

8

1 🔊037 Listen and match.　　**2** Trace.

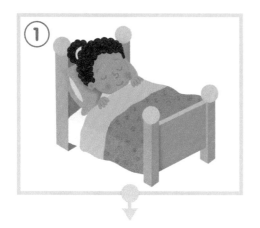

①

②

③

④

in the morning

in the afternoon

in the evening

at night

Lesson 7 Song　　**Language focus:** *When do you (brush your teeth)? In the morning / afternoon / evening. At night.*

1 Count and write.　2 Trace and say.

1	moon	
	stars	
	raccoons	
	fox	
	bats	

1 Draw for you. Say. 2 Which letter is missing? Write.

i__ the mor__i__g   i__ the after__oo__   i__ the eve__i__g

1 🔊038 Listen, find, and join.   2 Say for you.

| in the morning | in the afternoon | in the evening | at night |

Clothes

1 🔊039 Listen, read, and match. 2 Circle the hats.

| It's rainy. | It's windy. | It's hot and sunny. | It's cold and sunny. |

1 🔊040 Listen and draw.　2 Write.

a skirt　a T-shirt　pants　shoes　shorts

p an t s　　shor___ ___　　___ ___oes　　a ___-shir___　　a ___ ___irt

9

This **fish is on a dish.**

That **sock is in the box.**

1 Look, read, and circle.

She's wearing a crayon hat.

She's wearing a crayon shirt.

He's wearing a yellow costume.

He's wearing a pink costume.

2 Draw your face. Color your costume and say.

Language focus: *party, costume, paper; Let's make (crayon costumes) / play.*

Lesson 4 Story

9

1 Read, match, and write.

shoe

so___ ___

sock

sh___ ___

box

b___ ___

I reuse things.

Value: reuse things **Language focus:** *We can reuse this (shoe).*

1 What comes **after** these numbers? Say and write.

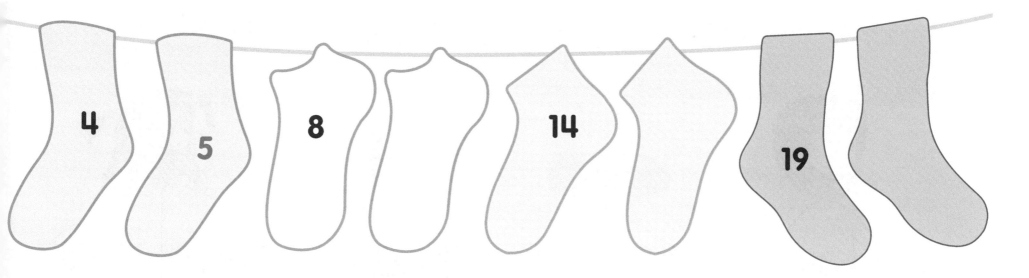

2 What comes **before** these numbers? Say and write.

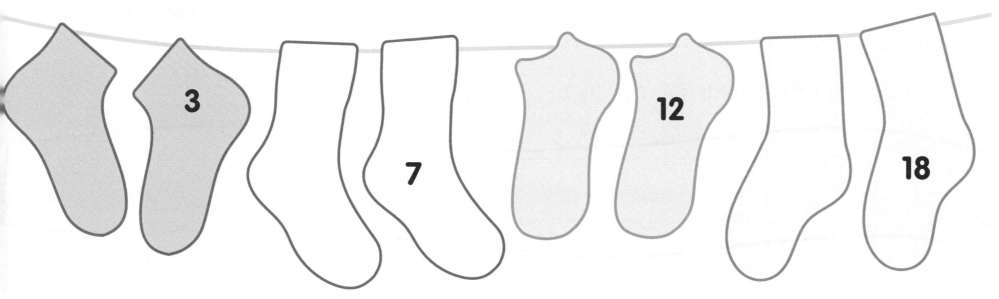

9

1 Color to match.   2 🔊 042 Listen and say.

scarf sweater **jacket** **dress**

① ② ③ ④

3 Find and trace the words from activity 1.

gadressoljacketnescarfintsweaterd

Lesson 7 Song   **Language focus:** *His/Her sweater / jacket / dress / scarf is too big / small.*

1 Match and say. **2** Trace.

3 Draw your pajamas. Write and say.

pajamas

swimsuit

apron

I'm wearing __a__a__a__.

1 Look, read, and match.

He's wearing a costume.

She's wearing pajamas.

He's wearing a sweater, pants, and shoes.

Language focus: *She's/He's wearing (a T-shirt). It's (red).*

1 Find, color, and write.   2 🔊043 Listen and circle.

dress   jacket   pants   shorts   skirt   sweater

 sw_e_ a_ t_ e_ r

 _ _ _ss

 sh_ _ _ _s

 _ _nt_

 _ _ck_ _

 _ _ir_

1 What's different in picture B? Circle six things.   2 🔊 044 Listen and say *A* or *B*.

1 Look and number.   2 Write.

hair
head
seeds
soil
water

h___ ___ r

s___ ___ ___ s

w___ ___ ___ r

s___ ___ l

1

h___ ___ d

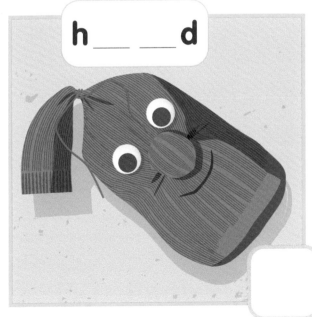

1 What does Elsa's dad make from her dress? Match and trace.

a scarf

a costume

pants

a shirt

shorts

a skirt

2 Do you like the story? Color.

No, I don't. ☹

1	2	3	4	5	6	7	8	9	10

☺ **Yes, I do.**

1 Read, draw, and color.

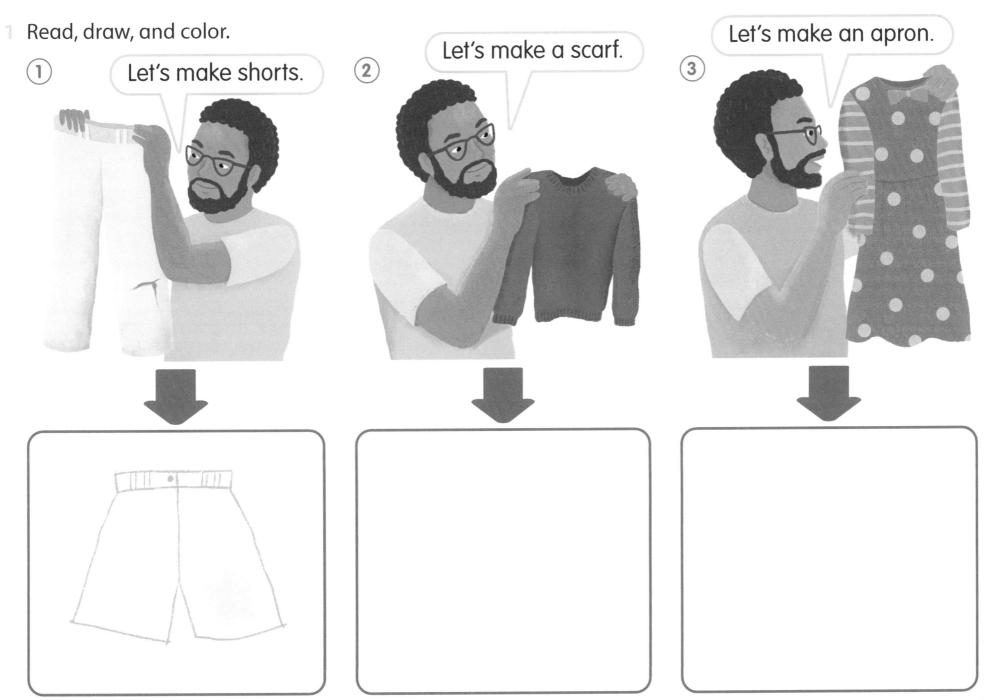

① Let's make shorts.

② Let's make a scarf.

③ Let's make an apron.

Great Clarendon Street, Oxford, OX2 6DP, United Kingdom

Oxford University Press is a department of the University of Oxford.
It furthers the University's objective of excellence in research, scholarship,
and education by publishing worldwide. Oxford is a registered trade
mark of Oxford University Press in the UK and in certain other countries

ISBN: 978 0 19 486290 5

Printed in Great Britain by Bell and Bain Ltd, Glasgow

This book is printed on paper from certified and well-managed sources

ACKNOWLEDGEMENTS

Illustrations by: Claudio Cerri/Beehive Illustration, pp.5, 7, 14, 17, 24, 27,
34, 36, 43, 50, 53, 60, 63, 70, 79, 89, 96, 99, 106; Helen Graper/Beehive
Illustration, pp.6, 16, 23, 26, 32, 37, 41, 48, 52, 58, 62, 72, 78, 82, 85, 94, 100,
105, 108; Hannah McCaffery/The Bright Agency, pp.74, 75; Veronica Montoya
Agulló/Advocate Art, p.38; Ed Myer/Advocate Art, pp.11, 20, 22, 31, 33, 39, 44,
45, 47, 57, 59, 64, 67, 73, 84, 87, 90, 93, 103; Kevin Payne/Advocate Art, pp.9,
19, 29, 45, 54, 55, 65, 81, 83, 91, 101; Mark Ruffle, pp.13, 21, 49, 69, 95, 109;
Angelika Scudamore/Advocate Art, pp.4, 10, 15, 25, 30, 35, 40, 46, 51, 56, 61,
66, 68, 76, 92, 97, 104, 107; Noopur Thakur/Advocate Art, pp.110, 111.

*The publisher would like to thank the following for permission to reproduce
photographs*: Getty Images (Capuski/E+, Jose Luis Pelaez, Inc., Demerzel21,
Tim Hall/Photodisc, JGI/Jamie Grill, Onebluelight/E+, Terry Vine/DigitalVision,
Oliver Rossi/DigitalVision, George Doyle/Stockbyte, RichLegg/E+);
Shutterstock (Iceink, USBFCO, Viktar Malyshchyts, M Kunz, Shutterstock,
Leestudio, Independent birds, All_about_people, Gilmar, Boris Bajkic,
Nopparada samrhubsuk, Aksenova Natalya, VICUSCHKA, Tsekhmister,
Dave Denby Photography, Volodymyr Burdiak, Ziga Amerik, Jud Goodwin,
Olha Afanasieva, Still AB, Anna Lurye, Lukas Gojda, Bitt24, Poylock19,
Maxbelchenk, Wirestock Creators, Ljupco Smokovski, Denis Kovin, Luma
Creative, Nigel Paul Monckton, Daniel Schoenen, Ajt, Fivespots, Manuel
Findies, Roblna, samrhubsuk, Josefauer, Ollyy, Nynke van Holten, New
Africa, Lightfield Studios, Brian A Jackson, FamVeld, rSnapshotPhotos,
Luciana Rinaldi, Roman Babakin, Slimstyl, Roman Babakin, Eric Isselee,
New Africa, Aksenova Natalya, Jocic, The Old Major, Eduardo Estellez,
Joe Kirby Photography, Vovantarakan, Gmlykin, Gunnar Pippel, New
Africa, Just2shutter, Eric Isselee, Gregory Gerber, Gmlykin, Yevgeniy11,
SUKJAI Photo, Irina Wilhauk, MIA Studio, Pressmaster, Jayakri, Drakuliren,
Hxdbzxy, Keith Publicover, Elnur, Africa Studio, Anna Lovnik, Photomaster,
G_O_S, PeopleImages.com-Yuri A, Ground Picture, Martin Mecnarowski,
PeopleImages.com – Yuri A, Angela Reichstein, Drazen Zigic, FotoRequest,
New Africa, Yevgeniy11, Mikhail Melnikov, noBorders – Brayden Howie,
Volurol, Pepers, Mega Pixel, Dmitry Kazitsyn, LightField Studios, Richard
Griffin, Richard Peterson, Maya Kruchankova).

Cover: Shutterstock (artjazz, Avesun, cz, Kitsana1980, piyaphon, Vandathai,
Eric Isselee, I am adventure, klyaksun, lewalp, nelik, Press master, sevenke,
SergiyN, Steve Best TukkataMoji).

Title page: Shutterstock (nelik).